PROVEN

PROVEN

A 31-DAY DEVOTIONAL

ON THE

BOOK

OF

JAMES

By RICK BURGESS

Published by Iron Hill Press

Published by:

PROVEN: A 31-Day Devotional on the Book of James

Published by Iron Hill Press in the United States of America.

Library of Congress Cataloging-in-Publication Data is on file
at the Library of Congress, Washington, DC.

ISBN: 978-1-970539-02-8

Cover design by Faceout Studio, Brian Mellema.

TABLE OF CONTENTS

INTRODUCTION

BEING A CHRIST-FOLLOWER ISN'T EASY.

That fact shouldn't come as a surprise, considering that Jesus told us as much in His Word. In Matthew 7:13–14, Jesus tells us that the path that leads to life is narrow and difficult, while the path that leads to destruction is wide and easy. In John 15:18–19, Jesus tells us not to be surprised if the world hates us, because it hated Him first! In John 16:33, Jesus reminds us that in this world, we *will* have trouble (not that we *might*) before encouraging us to take heart, knowing that He has already overcome the world.

Faith, by its very nature, will be tested. And tested faith is proven faith.

Living out our faith, especially as men, can be challenging. Now, it's also the most rewarding life we can live! But it isn't easy. It is no easy task for a man to die to self and faithfully follow Jesus, day in and day out. But that's the issue James touches on: real faith doesn't hide in comfort. It is revealed under pressure.

Which is precisely why we don't need another soft message telling us to play it safe, or to keep our heads down and hope things work out. Men are in desperate need of the truth. Men need a challenge. We need to be held to a higher standard, to live as men of God in a world that constantly tries to pull us off course.

We don't need a faith that only sounds good. We need a faith that is proven. And there are few better sources for this task than the Book of James.

If you've read this powerful little book before, you know that the Book of James doesn't waste time with theory or fluff. It's more like a battle manual for our everyday faith. I love how James gets straight to the point: if you claim to follow Jesus, then your life ought to show it. That's pretty simple, isn't it, brother?

Faith is not simply what we say we believe. The world is full of people who claim to believe in Jesus. But their lives don't support their words. A true faith must be a faith of works, not to earn salvation, but as evidence of it. An authentic, saving faith is evident in how we speak, how we handle temptation, how we treat others, and how we persevere when life challenges us. Because make no mistake, it will.

James was the half-brother of Jesus. (Let that sink in for a bit.) But he wasn't always a believer. This man, who would later become the leader of the Jerusalem Church, grew up in Jesus' house and still didn't believe until after the resurrection. But when James finally put his faith in Christ, he became a bold leader. He completely understood the cost of discipleship. He watched believers, his brothers and sisters in Christ, scattered by persecution and struggling to hold onto hope in a hostile world. That's the world he wrote into, and his words hit just as hard today as they did 2,000 years ago. And he wrote to men and women whose faith was being tested, not in theory, but in real suffering, because the testing is where faith is either proven or exposed.

Why the Book of James Speaks to Men

If there's one thing men respect, it's straight talk. I value it in my life, and I feel confident you do as well. I don't want a pep rally when it comes to someone leading me in my faith. I don't need sugarcoating. I want someone to hand me the playbook, look me in the eye, and say, "Here's what it takes to make this happen." How about you?

If you're like me, you'll appreciate James. Because that's exactly how his book is written.

In five short chapters, James calls men to real, visible, tested faith. He tells us to face trials head-on, because trials produce endurance. He warns us that temptation is real, but God always provides a way out. He challenges us to control our tongues, to humble ourselves before God, to resist the devil, and to live with patience and perseverance until Christ returns. He reminds us that prayer is powerful and that brotherhood is essential.

Every page of James cuts against the grain of comfortable, cultural Christianity. James won't let us hide behind excuses or half-hearted religion. He drags faith out of mere ideas and forces it out into the open, where it either stands strong or collapses under pressure. And that's exactly what men need today.

What You'll Take Away

Over the next several weeks, you'll walk through James one section at a time. Each devotional is crafted directly from Scripture and tied to real-life experiences. You're going to hear hard truths because James doesn't let us off the hook. But I also believe you'll encounter hope, because every challenge James gives us is matched with the promise of God's presence, strength, and reward.

Here's what you'll discover as you go:

- **Faith under fire produces endurance.** The trials we face aren't meant to crush us; they are meant to strengthen us. God allows us to undergo tough times in order to refine us into stronger, steadier men of God.
- **Spiritual strength is forged in hardship.** Endurance isn't built in comfort. It's built-in resistance. James calls men to stay in the fight when others quit.
- **Your words reveal your heart.** James shows us how our speech (to our wives, our kids, our coworkers, etc.) flows directly out of our faith.
- **Pride kills, but humility wins.** God opposes the proud but gives grace to the humble. Men who submit to God and resist the devil walk in victory.
- **Brotherhood matters.** James ends his letter by reminding us that restoring a wandering brother is a matter of life and death. Men are not meant to fight alone.

Brother, this isn't a casual read. If you engage with these devotionals, they will confront you, convict you, and push you to grow. But they'll also encourage you, because the God who calls you to endure is the same God who equips you with His Spirit to endure.

Why It Matters

Would you agree that we live in a culture that applauds comfort, compromise, and passivity? Men are constantly told to back off and be silent. But the Word of God says otherwise. James calls men to rise up and to live with conviction, endurance, and humility in a world that desperately needs examples of godly manhood.

This study through James is about more than filling your head with knowledge. It's about transformation. It's about letting the Word of God expose the places where your faith is weak and challenging you to put it into action. It's about learning to persevere when life gets hard and to pray with boldness when you're tempted to give up.

James doesn't leave room for half measures. Neither should we.

So here's the challenge: lean in. Read each devotional with an ear tuned to the Holy Spirit's leading. Wrestle with the questions. Talk honestly with other men. And most importantly, act on what you read.

Brother, this is faith that works and endures. This is a faith that is proven. This is the kind of faith men need today.

DAY 1

AN INTRODUCTION TO JAMES

"But be doers of the word, and not hearers only, deceiving yourselves."
—JAMES 1:22

IF YOU WERE TO SUM UP the Book of James in one sentence, it might sound like this: *Faith that doesn't work isn't faith at all.* That's the heartbeat of his letter. James, the half-brother of Jesus, isn't writing his letter to the world. Instead, he's writing to believers who claim the name of Jesus but aren't living like it. He's calling out a kind of hollow, surface-level religion that talks big but produces nothing real.

James doesn't play around. He's not here to tickle ears. He's here to test hearts. The entire Book of James is a spiritual stress test. It shows whether our faith is genuine or just a label we wear. Real faith, according to James, leaves fingerprints. It shows up in what we do, how we speak, how we treat people, how we suffer, and how we obey.

And let's just get this out of the way now (though we'll revisit it in detail later): James isn't trying to add works to salvation. What James says is that salvation naturally produces works. He's not contradicting Paul, who wrote that we are saved by grace through faith. He's completing the picture. Paul tells us how we *come* to faith; James tells us what that faith *looks* like when it's genuine. If your faith hasn't changed how you live, you might need to ask if you really have it.

Throughout this book, James challenges believers to match their confession with their conduct and to walk out what they claim to believe. He calls us to a rugged, practical Christianity that refuses to hide behind words. Because the truth is, the world doesn't need more people talking about Jesus. What the world needs is more people living like Him.

Brother, as we study James, the question before us isn't *"What do you believe?"* Instead, it's *"What does your life prove about what you believe"*?

Application Questions

1. How would you describe the difference between saying you have faith and showing it?
2. What areas of your life reveal evidence that your faith is genuine?
3. Where might God be challenging you to move from belief to obedience?
4. How could your daily actions better reflect the faith you claim?

A Prayer for Your Day

Father, I don't want to just *talk* about faith; I want to *live* it. Teach me to be a doer of Your Word, not just a hearer. Expose any hypocrisy in me, and give me the courage to obey You completely. Let my life prove that my faith is genuine. Amen.

DAY 2

JOY IN THE FIRE

"Count it all joy, my brothers, when you meet trials of various kinds, for you know that the testing of your faith produces steadfastness. And let steadfastness have its full effect, that you may be perfect and complete, lacking in nothing."

—JAMES 1:2–4

READ JAMES 1:2–4. James opens his letter with a command that feels almost impossible: find joy in trials. This is what is known as a paradox, a statement that appears to contradict itself. How can a person find joy in the midst of trials? Before we get to that, let's take notice of the fact that James doesn't say "if" trials come, but "when." Brother, our struggles are not an interruption to life; our struggles are woven into it. I have had my fair share of hardships, and I bet you have too. Trials are a part of our lives.

Here's something even more profound: For the Christ-follower, our trials are not random. They are purposeful.

The Bible tells us that God allows trials in order to strengthen and grow our faith. However, it's not as if God is trying to make us fail. In the same way gold is refined in fire, where the dross is burned away, God refines our faith in trials. Pressure, heat, and time reveal what is genuine and burn away what is weak. In God's hands, hardship becomes the forge where steadfastness is formed. And steadfastness (a fruit of the Spirit, by the way) makes us mature men, complete men, men who lack nothing.

Brother, this is why James can call us to joy in the midst of our trials. He does not call us to joy in the pain itself, that would be cruel and even impossible, but joy in the God who works through it. Trials are evidence that God is shaping us into people who can stand firm in Him, no matter what comes. Every difficulty becomes a tool in God's hand to strengthen our endurance and deepen our trust. Ultimately, God uses our trials to make us more like Jesus.

The call here is profoundly countercultural. We don't have to look very far to see that our world tells us to avoid suffering at all costs, treating comfort as the highest good. Yet James says trials are not wasted. Instead, they are invitations to grow. This doesn't mean we paste on fake smiles in hardship. It means we anchor our hope in the truth that God is at work, and we trust that He will complete what He has started.

Application Questions

1. How do you typically respond when trials enter your life? Do you react with resistance or with trust in God's purposes?
2. Can you identify a time when a difficult season actually strengthened your faith or deepened your character?
3. What would it look like to choose joy in the middle of your current struggles? Describe what this looks like in your own life.
4. How can you remind yourself daily that God uses trials to produce endurance?

A Prayer for Your Day

Father, thank You for reminding me that the hard things in my life are not wasted. When the pressure feels heavy and the fire feels hot, help me remember that You are refining me, not forsaking me. Teach me to find joy, not in the struggle itself, but in Your strength at work within it. Make me a steadfast man who doesn't quit, who trusts You when life gets hard, and who grows to look more like Jesus through every trial. Amen.

DAY 3

ASKING GOD FOR WISDOM

"If any of you lacks wisdom, let him ask God, who gives generously to all without reproach, and it will be given him."
— JAMES 1:5

READ JAMES 1:5–8. Trials have a way of exposing our limits. When life becomes overwhelming, most of us quickly realize that we don't have all the answers. Any thought that we have control over our lives fades fast when the pressure rises. That's why James' encouragement hits home. When you don't know what to do, God says to ask Him for wisdom, and He will provide.

Don't be deceived: This isn't us just asking God for more information or insight. Biblical wisdom is the God-given skill of living faithfully in the real world. Think about that for a moment. Biblical wisdom is knowing how to respond when the diagnosis comes, the deal falls through, a loved one's life is cut short, or the relationship fractures. Wisdom is discernment in action. It is the ability to align your choices with God's will when the next step feels unclear.

Here's the good news, brother: God isn't stingy with wisdom. James says He "gives generously to all without reproach." In other words, God isn't frustrated with our confusion or impatient with our questions. He isn't like some of the people we know; He doesn't roll His eyes when we come back again and again asking for clarity. God delights to guide His children. I'm not sure about you, but I have relied on this truth time and again in my life, and God has never let me down.

But James also includes a warning: asking for wisdom must be accompanied by faith. He describes the one who doubts as a man who is "like a wave of the sea, driven and tossed by the wind." When we approach God's wisdom as just one option among many, as if His way might not hold up in real life, we become unstable, easily swayed by emotions or circumstances. The kind of wisdom God provides requires trust. It means saying, "God, whatever You show me, I'll follow it."

The truth is, this is where many of us stumble. This is definitely where I stumbled in my past, as an immature and uncommitted Christian. I wanted God's wisdom, but I preferred it on my own terms, which, let's be honest, really isn't wisdom at all. Often, we want God to provide guidance that just affirms or aligns with our comfort zones. But the kind of wisdom God gives doesn't usually work that way. God's wisdom calls us to courage, humility, and obedience. The wisdom He gives stretches us beyond ourselves.

Brother, the call of James 1:5 is an invitation to that deeper trust. The same God who saved you through faith in the person and work of Jesus will never withhold the wisdom you need to walk faithfully through what you're facing today. Ask Him and trust Him. Then, move forward in the wisdom He *will* provide.

Application Questions

1. Where in your life right now do you feel most in need of God's wisdom?
2. When you ask God for guidance, do you truly trust His answers? Or do you find yourself keeping backup plans?
3. How does believing in God's generosity (v.5) change the way you approach Him in prayer?
4. What would it look like this week to act on God's wisdom rather than leaning on your own understanding?

A Prayer for Your Day

Father, I admit that I don't always know what to do. There are moments when I'm unsure. But You promise wisdom to those who ask, and You promise to give it generously. So I'm asking You now to teach me to see things the way You see them. Give me the courage to trust what You show me, even when it's hard or uncomfortable. Forgive me for the times I've wanted Your guidance without surrendering my will. Make me a man who seeks Your wisdom first, who believes it fully, and who walks in it faithfully. Amen.

DAY 4

TRUE RICHES IN CHRIST

"Let the lowly brother boast in his exaltation,
and the rich in his humiliation, because like a flower of the grass
he will pass away. For the sun rises with its scorching heat and
withers the grass; its flower falls, and its beauty perishes.
So also will the rich man fade away in the midst of his pursuits."
— JAMES 1:9–11

READ JAMES 1:9–11. One of the reasons I love the Book of James is that it completely flips the world's values upside down. The lowly Christ-follower, the one who is overlooked and under-resourced, is told to "boast in his exaltation." Why? Because in Jesus, I am adopted as God's son. The outcast is seated with Christ! The man who has nothing on earth has everything in heaven. In Jesus, no matter how small our worldly status, we are made heirs of eternal riches. In the Kingdom of God, our worth isn't measured by our paycheck, or our platform, or even our possessions. The true measure of our worth is the life Jesus purchased for us through His blood on the cross. That truth alone should anchor our identity.

But James doesn't stop there. He turns his attention to the wealthy believer, telling him to "boast in his humiliation." That always sounded counterintuitive to me. But James isn't condemning money itself. Instead, he's reminding us of something we already know: that money *does* something to men's hearts. Wealth tells us lies of self-sufficiency, especially to men. It can make a man think he doesn't need God as much as he actually does. James reminds us that earthly riches fade like weeds scorched by the summer sun. What once looked so good and full of promise soon withers and disappears. Never forget, brother, that everything this world offers—money, status, success, etc.—is temporary.

James' point isn't to glorify poverty or to shame those who have been prosperous. What he's trying to do is help shift our perspective. Whether you have much or little, you are called to boast in Christ alone. Never forget, brother, that God's economy doesn't run on dollars or titles. God's economy runs on grace. He measures our value by our faith in Jesus, not by anything we have or haven't done on this earth.

Everything in this world, our position, our possessions, and even our outward appearance, will fade away. But what is rooted in Jesus will never die. The only secure treasure is what is stored up in heaven. So, whether life finds you in a season of abundance or lack, learn to hold it all with open hands. Find your joy not in what you have, but in whose you are.

The question James presses on each of us is a simple one, yet one that will rock you to your core: *Is Jesus enough for you?*

Application Questions

1. When you think about your identity, do you tend to measure it by worldly success or by your standing in Christ?
2. How might God be asking you to hold loosely to money, status, or possessions?
3. What practical steps could you take this week to "boast in Christ" rather than in achievements or resources?
4. How would your perspective shift if you regularly reminded yourself that everything in this life will fade, but Christ remains?

A Prayer for Your Day

Father, remind me today that everything I have can fade, but who I am in You will never change. Keep me from chasing security in things that can't last. Whether You've given me much or little, help me to see it all as grace and to hold it loosely. Teach me to find my worth in Jesus alone, not in what I earn, achieve, or own. Give me the courage to boast only in Christ, and the wisdom to live like He's truly enough for me. Amen.

DAY 5

THE CROWN OF LIFE

"Blessed is the man who remains steadfast under trial, for when he has stood the test he will receive the crown of life, which God has promised to those who love him."
—JAMES 1:12

READ JAMES 1:12–15. James reminds us that our trials, though painful, lead to blessings for those who remain steadfast. The "crown of life" he describes isn't a simple trinket. Instead, it's the reward of eternal life and deep fellowship with God. Being steadfast under trials isn't about earning salvation but about proving the genuineness of our faith. Our endurance under pressure reveals our love for God, and that love produces joy that outlasts hardship. That's a truth you can bank on.

But James also draws a sharp line between trials and temptations. Trials come from the outside. Trials are things like pressure from the world, loss, and hardship. As we have already discussed, they are permitted by God to strengthen and refine us. Temptation, on the other hand, comes from the inside. God never tempts anyone to sin. Temptation takes root when our desires fix on something outside God's will. James tells us that, left unchecked, those desires give birth to sin, and sin, when full-grown, leads to death.

I don't know how to put it any more plainly: the testing of our faith is meant for good; temptation is bent toward evil. God uses trials to purify and strengthen us, while temptation seeks to destroy us. And yet, even in that warning, there's great hope. James is telling us to see temptation for what it really is: a chain that starts with desire and ends in destruction. The earlier we recognize it, the easier it is to resist it.

Brother, we've got to stop excusing sin as if we're powerless against it. Don't fool yourself; when you sin, it's because you want to, plain and simple. The devil can tempt, but he can't make us fall. Most of our battles aren't with

Satan; they're with our own desires. But here's the good news: the same power that raised Jesus from the dead lives in us. We are not helpless. The Spirit of God gives us strength to endure trials and overcome temptation.

When temptation to sin wells up in you, run from it. Turn to God and ask Him to lead you out of it. He is faithful and He will always provide a way out (1 Cor. 10:13). Remember, endurance builds steadfast men, and steadfast men of God receive the crown of life.

Application Questions

1. What trials are you facing right now that require steadfastness? How can you endure in love for God?
2. Where are you most vulnerable to temptation, and how can you recognize the early stages of desire before it grows?
3. What does the "crown of life" mean to you, and how does it give you hope?
4. How does knowing that God never tempts us change the way you view your struggles with sin?

A Prayer for Your Day

Father, I thank You that every trial I face has a purpose. When life presses hard against me, remind me that You're not trying to break me; You're shaping me. Give me the strength to stand firm when the heat turns up and the courage to trust You through it. When temptation rises from within, open my eyes to see it for what it is and give me the wisdom to turn away before it takes root. Teach me to rely on Your Spirit, not my strength. Make me a steadfast man who endures with love, obedience, and faith until the end. Amen.

DAY 6

EVERY GOOD AND PERFECT GIFT

"Do not be deceived, my beloved brothers. Every good gift and every perfect gift is from above, coming down from the Father of lights, with whom there is no variation or shadow due to change. Of his own will he brought us forth by the word of truth, that we should be a kind of firstfruits of his creatures."
— JAMES 1:16–18

READ JAMES 1:16–18. In this passage, James issues a warning that every man needs to hear: *"Do not be deceived."* Sin not only tempts us, it lies to us. Temptation whispers to us that our satisfaction, our desire to control, or even our purpose can be found apart from God. But James is calling us to remember that there is a truth that we cannot deny: every good and perfect gift comes from God. Everything that truly satisfies, peace, love, purpose, forgiveness, etc., flows from the unchanging hand of God. That is a truth that is easy to overlook, but one that we should constantly keep in mind.

James then turns our focus to the character of the Giver. God, James says, is not moody. He doesn't shift like shadows or waver in His goodness. When our circumstances change, His nature is constant. He is dependable and steady. Have you experienced this, brother? Have you seen God's steady hand of provision and care in the midst of life's many trials?

In a world where everything else moves, God does not. That's good news. When life shakes us, God remains the same. His goodness doesn't rise and fall with the temperature of our obedience. He gives because it's who He is: the Father of lights who never changes.

And don't forget that the greatest proof of His goodness isn't something material. It's that He chose to make us new. "Of His own will," James says, "He brought us forth by the word of truth." Never forget this truth, brother.

God wanted us. That's a staggering reality. Our salvation wasn't a backup plan or a response to our efforts. It was God's will. It was His decision. It was His gift. Through the Gospel, God gives us new life so that we can become the "firstfruits" of His creation, set apart as living evidence of His goodness and grace. I pray that we never grow cold to this truth.

So, brother, when life tempts you to doubt God's goodness, pause and remember who He is. Look around at the blessings you've been given, for they are many. Your salvation, your family, your health, your next breath, etc. Let gratitude be present in your life.

Every good thing in your life can be traced back to a faithful Father who never changes. Never forget this!

Application Questions

1. How does remembering God as the source of "every good gift" shape your gratitude?
2. What gifts has God given you recently that you may have overlooked?
3. How does God's unchanging character give you confidence in uncertain seasons?
4. What does it mean to you personally that God willed to make you His "firstfruits"?

A Prayer for Your Day

Father, thank You for being steady when everything else shifts. Help me see every good thing in my life as a gift from You, not something I earned or deserve. When I'm tempted to chase satisfaction apart from You, remind me that You alone are the source of what's good and lasting. Teach me to live with gratitude, to trust Your character, and to reflect Your goodness in how I live today. Amen.

DAY 7

HEARING AND DOING

"Know this, my beloved brothers: let every person be quick to hear, slow to speak, slow to anger; for the anger of man does not produce the righteousness of God. Therefore put away all filthiness and rampant wickedness and receive with meekness the implanted word, which is able to save your souls. But be doers of the word, and not hearers only, deceiving yourselves."

— JAMES 1:19–22

READ JAMES 1:19–27. James closes this section of his letter with a call to action that hits right where most men live. James does what he does best here. He's not speaking in theory; he's describing the kind of faith that's real and practical. James calls us to a genuine faith that listens before it speaks and keeps its temper under control. He calls us to be men who receive God's truth with humility. That's the mark of a man transformed by grace.

I love the wording James uses here. He says the Word of God is "implanted." This means that it's been placed deep within us by the Holy Spirit. The relationship with the Word that the Spirit makes possible isn't a surface-level one. It's a genuine connection with the living and active Word of God, a Word that is capable of shaping our thoughts, desires, and behavior. But that transformation only happens when we welcome it, when we partner with the Spirit to open ourselves up to being moved by the Word.

Brother, make no mistake, we must let the Word take root and bear fruit in our lives. Too often, men treat Scripture like background noise rather than the foundation of our lives. We hear sermons, podcasts, or Bible readings but fail to let them truly shape our lives.

As I encounter men across the country, I hear stories of men who have fallen in love with the Bible, and I hear stories of men who make excuses for not having done so. The truth of the matter is that far too many men have a passing relationship with the Bible, hearing it, but not doing it. James says that's self-deception, and he is, of course, correct. He compares it to looking in a mirror and then forgetting what you look like, an absurd notion. God's Word reveals to us who we are, including both the flaws we'd rather not face and the potential of who we can become in Jesus. But if we walk away unchanged, we've missed the point.

Don't forget, James isn't talking about our salvation. He's talking about proving the reality of our faith through our obedience. Real faith produces fruit. We know this. That's why James says the one who "looks into the perfect law . . . and perseveres" will be blessed. God doesn't bless us when we passively listen to the Word. He blesses us when we engage deeply and actively obey.

Our world doesn't need more men who can give lip service to Scripture. Our world desperately needs men who *live* it.

My challenge to you today is to let God's Word move from your ears to your hands, and from your mind to your mouth. Hear the Word, believe the Word, and put the Word to work in your life!

Application Questions

1. What practical step can you take this week to let God's Word move from the surface of your life to the center, where it can actually take root and change you?
2. Be honest: Are there areas where you've been hearing God's truth but not living it out? What would obedience look like in those specific areas?
3. If someone watched your life this week, what evidence would they see that you're not just a hearer of the Word but a doer? What one action can you take today to live out your faith more boldly?

A Prayer for Your Day

Father, thank You for giving me your Word, not just to hear, but to live. Plant Your truth deep in my heart so that it takes root and changes the way I think, speak, and act. I don't want to just know Your Word; I want to live it. Teach me to be a man who obeys You in the small things and the big ones. Amen.

DAY 8

FAITH AND FAVORITISM

"My brothers, show no partiality as you hold the faith in our Lord Jesus Christ, the Lord of glory."
— JAMES 2:1

READ JAMES 2:1–4. Chapter 2 starts with James being James. He wastes no time before cutting straight to a hard truth: favoritism has no place among God's people.

In these verses, James paints the picture of a church service where a wealthy, well-dressed man walks in, and all eyes are on him. You can just see him now, can't you? He's offered the best seat and the warmest welcome. But right behind him comes a poor man in shabby clothes. He's disheveled and rough-looking. And he's quickly pushed aside and told to sit on the floor. With this as the backdrop, James asks, "Have you not then made distinctions among yourselves and become judges with evil thoughts?"

This passage reveals how easily our flesh is drawn to the powerful and impressive. We might never say it out loud, but deep down, we often equate status with value. Picture yourself watching a Friday night football game, making your way through the bleachers to pick a seat. There is an open seat beside a homeless-looking man and another open seat beside a man who looks like he's stepped out of a GQ magazine. Who would most people find themselves sitting next to? Most people would likely choose to avoid the shabbily dressed man. But James says that when we do this, we are not living as people shaped by the Gospel. We're playing favorites based on the world's standards instead of God's.

What's striking here is that James writes this to Christ-followers. Even in the early church, prejudice, partiality, and class divisions threatened to fracture the fellowship of God's people. But the Gospel levels the playing field. At the cross, every one of us stands equally needy of grace, equally dependent on Jesus' sacrifice. To exalt one brother while belittling another is to deny the very heart of the Gospel.

This isn't just about seating charts in church. Favoritism is evident in the people we spend time with, the ones we invest in, the ones we invite into our homes, and the ones we choose to ignore. It creeps into how we view coworkers, how we talk about our neighbors, and how we treat those who can give us nothing in return. James doesn't mince words. He reminds us that favoritism is a spiritual failure, not just a small social slip. It reveals hearts that are still shaped more by the world's values than by God's truth.

As followers of Christ, we're called to see others through the lens of the Gospel, not through the lens of wealth, status, or appearance. What lens are you more inclined to use?

Application Questions

1. Where in your life are you tempted to show favoritism: at work, in your neighborhood, or even at church?
2. How does the cross challenge the way you view people who are different from you?
3. What steps could you take this week to intentionally honor someone who may feel overlooked?
4. How does favoritism undermine the unity Jesus desires for His people?

A Prayer for Your Day

Father, forgive me for the times I've shown favoritism, the times when I've judged people by what they have, how they look, or what they can do for me. Help me to see others the way You see them: through the lens of the cross. Remind me that every person I meet bears Your image and is someone You love deeply. Teach me to honor others without condition, to serve without expecting anything in return, and to reflect Your grace in the way I treat people. Shape my heart to look more like Yours. Amen.

DAY 9

GOD'S KINGDOM ECONOMY

"Listen, my beloved brothers, has not God chosen those who are poor in the world to be rich in faith and heirs of the kingdom, which he has promised to those who love him?"

— JAMES 2:5

READ JAMES 2:5–7. Today's passage builds upon the verses we read yesterday. In James 2:5–7, the author shifts from exposing favoritism to explaining why it's so out of step with God's ways. "Listen, my beloved brothers, has not God chosen those who are poor in the world to be rich in faith and heirs of the kingdom?" James asks. What is James getting at here?

James is helping us see that God doesn't measure worth the way the world does. The world idolizes wealth, power, and influence. But God often works through the overlooked and the humble. God exalts those who are despised by culture, and James says that He makes them heirs of His Kingdom. The irony is that the very people the church was tempted to favor, the rich and powerful, were often the same ones oppressing believers (v.6). James reminds his audience that they are dishonoring the poor man while cozying up to those who blaspheme the very name of Jesus (v.7). This kind of sin is a betrayal of the Gospel itself.

Brother, don't miss this. There's a piercing application here for us. We live in a culture that worships success stories, influencers, and high achievers. But the economy of God's Kingdom flips the script. Riches of our faith matter more than the riches of the world. Often, those who may seem insignificant are the ones most treasured by God.

Think about Jesus Himself. Our Savior was born in a manger. He was raised in obscurity. He was rejected by the powerful. Yet He is the King of Kings and Lord of Lords! When the church reflects the values of the world instead of the values of Christ, it loses its witness to the world.

For men, this raises questions about how we define success. Is it the size of our paycheck, the prestige of our title, or the respect of the community? Or is it the depth of our faith and the way we live out our calling as heirs of God's Kingdom? James calls us back to reality: true wealth is found in faith, and true honor is found in belonging to Christ.

Application Questions

1. Be honest: How do you usually measure success in your life? Does it align more with the world's economy or God's?
2. Why do you think God often chooses the weak and outcast to display His power?
3. How should this passage challenge the way we treat people who have little worldly status?
4. In what ways might you be tempted to value influence or wealth over faithfulness?

A Prayer for Your Day

Lord, help me to see people the way You do. Strip away my pride, my obsession with status, and my tendency to measure worth by the world's standards. Remind me that true success isn't found in wealth or achievement but in faithfulness to You. Give me a humble heart that honors others, especially those the world overlooks. May my life reflect the values of Your Kingdom, not those of my culture. Make me rich in faith and generous in love. Amen.

DAY 10

THE ROYAL LAW OF LOVE

"So speak and so act as those who are to be judged under the law of liberty. For judgment is without mercy to one who has shown no mercy. Mercy triumphs over judgment."
— JAMES 2:12–13

READ JAMES 2:8–13. James lays down a principle that cuts to the core of Christian living: "If you really fulfill the royal law according to the Scripture, 'You shall love your neighbor as yourself,' you are doing well" (v.8). Favoritism is exposed not just as a social misstep but as a violation of God's law of love.

Notice the language: *royal law.* James doesn't tell us that love is not optional. He doesn't say that it's a suggestion. James assures us that love is the supreme command that governs the way we live as citizens of God's Kingdom. To show partiality to anyone, James says, is to sin and be convicted by the law (v.9). Even if we keep the rest of God's law, to break this one is to become guilty of all (v.10).

This is heavy, brothers. James is reminding believers that sin isn't just about the "big things" like murder or adultery. It's about any failure to love as God has commanded. Consider that for a moment when we think about how we treat our wives, our children, our friends, and perhaps especially strangers. When we choose to honor one person while despising another, we're breaking the heart of God's law.

But James doesn't leave us there. He points us to mercy. "So speak and so act as those who are to be judged under the law of liberty. For judgment is without mercy to one who has shown no mercy. Mercy triumphs over judgment" (vs.12–13). The Gospel of Jesus Christ frees us from condemnation, but it also frees us to love others with the same mercy God has shown us. And I don't know about you, but I am fully aware of the mercy God has shown me!

We live under the law of liberty, the freedom of being forgiven and accepted in Christ. That freedom isn't an excuse to sin; it's an invitation to live out a radical mercy to those in most need of it. For us, this means that the measure we use toward others, whether that is mercy or judgment, reveals the reality of our own faith. If we truly know the mercy of Christ, we will extend mercy to others. And when we fail, we return to the cross, where mercy triumphed once and for all.

Application Questions

1. Why does James call love the "royal law"? How does that elevate its importance in the Christian life?
2. How does showing favoritism to others break the law of love?
3. In your relationships, are you quicker to judge or to extend mercy? Why do you think that is?
4. How does remembering God's mercy toward you free you to show mercy to others?

A Prayer for Your Day

Father, thank You for the mercy You've shown me. It's mercy I could never earn and don't deserve. Help me remember that every person I meet is someone You've called me to love. Forgive me for the moments I've been quick to judge and slow to show grace. Teach me to live as a man shaped by Your mercy, not by pride or favoritism. Let my words and actions reflect the freedom and compassion I've found in Christ. Amen.

DAY 11

FAITH WITHOUT WORKS IS DEAD

"What good is it, my brothers, if someone says he has faith but does not have works? Can that faith save him?"
— JAMES 2:14

READ JAMES 2:14–17. James doesn't mince words here: "What good is it, my brothers, if someone says he has faith but does not have works? Can that faith save him?" (v.14). Now, let make sure we're super clear on what James is saying here. He's not denying salvation by grace through faith. He's not advocating for a works-based salvation. No, James is showing what *true* faith looks like. Real faith is faith that produces visible fruit.

James illustrates this truth with a simple, convicting example. Imagine seeing a brother or sister in need, perhaps they are lacking clothes or daily food, and you pat them on the back and say, "Hey, have an awesome day! Make sure you stay warm and get yourself a bite to eat," but do nothing to actually help. James asks bluntly, "What good is that?" (v.16). The answer is obvious: it's worthless.

This is where James draws his famous conclusion: "So also faith by itself, if it does not have works, is dead" (v.17). In other words, a faith that only talks but never acts is not faith at all. It's a corpse. It's dead. It's every bit as dead as a body in a morgue.

Brother, these words from James have served as a wake-up call for people for thousands of years. Do they wake you up? I hope they do. Too often, we treat Christianity as a set of beliefs we check off rather than a way of life that reshapes everything we do. James confronts this shallow version of faith. If your faith doesn't move you to compassion, generosity, obedience, righteousness, self-control, and holiness, then I have some very grave news for you: it isn't real faith.

This isn't about earning salvation; it's about evidence of salvation. Faith is the root; works are the fruit. You can't claim to have the root if there's never any fruit. James is calling us to a living, active, vibrant faith that shows itself in the way we treat people, in the way we serve, and in the way we obey God.

The world doesn't need men who talk about faith while living like everyone else. It needs men whose faith is alive, proven in action, even when it's costly and inconvenient. What kind of man are you?

Application Questions

1. How does James' example of ignoring a brother in need challenge the way you view your daily choices?
2. Where in your life might your faith be more talk than action?
3. Why is it important to distinguish between works as evidence of faith versus works as a way of earning salvation?
4. What specific act of obedience or compassion could you take this week to demonstrate a living faith?

A Prayer for Your Day

Lord, don't let my faith be hollow words or empty talk. Wake me up to live what I say I believe. Give me eyes to see the needs around me and hands ready to serve. Teach me to love with action, not just intention. I don't want to carry a faith that's dead; I want to live a faith that breathes Your life into everything I do. May my obedience be genuine and my compassion sincere, so that the world sees You in me. Amen.

DAY 12

SHOW ME YOUR FAITH

"But someone will say, 'You have faith and I have works.' Show me your faith apart from your works, and I will show you my faith by my works. You believe that God is one; you do well. Even the demons believe—and shudder! Do you want to be shown, you foolish person, that faith apart from works is useless?"

— JAMES 2:18–20

READ JAMES 2:18–20. Today, we continue our look at this well-known and often misunderstood passage of Scripture. Yesterday, we looked at James 2:14–17, where James makes a bold statement that faith that doesn't produce good works in us isn't faith at all. In today's verses, James anticipates the objection from his audience: "But someone will say, 'You have faith and I have works.'" His reply is cutting: "Show me your faith apart from your works, and I will show you my faith by my works" (v.18).

Wow. What James is saying here is that faith, if it's real, can be *seen.* We like to think about faith as something that is invisible. I can't hold my faith in my hands or put it under a microscope to examine it. But the fruit of our faith is unmistakable. When the Gospel takes root in a man's life, it always produces evidence. Our good works don't compete with our faith; they *complete* our faith. Faith that doesn't act isn't faith at all.

James goes further to expose hollow belief. "You believe that God is one; you do well. Even the demons believe—and shudder!" (v.19). That's a chilling line. The demons know the reality of God better than we do. After all, they've seen His power firsthand. But that knowledge doesn't produce obedience or love. It produces fear. In other words, it's entirely possible to believe all the right things about God and still not belong to Him. A "head knowledge" of God is not saving faith. The faith we see in the Bible isn't as simple as a knowledge of the truth. Biblical faith is *believing* the truth and responding with repentance from sin. This belief opens the door for the Holy Spirit to transform us into a new creation in Christ (Cor. 5:17). The new life we live is one lived in the power of the Spirit, in which He works in us to produce godliness and, through us, to produce righteous deeds. If there is no fruit of righteousness in our lives, we must ask, "Have we truly been redeemed by faith?"

James calls this kind of empty, fruitless belief "useless" (v.20). It's like a car with no engine or a body with no heartbeat. There's a body, but no life. The kind of faith that saves isn't passive; it works, it obeys, and it moves. James is helping us see that faith and works aren't two paths to God; they are one reality. Works are the natural overflow of genuine belief. If there are no works, then what we call "faith" isn't the kind that saves.

Brother, this passage should wake us up. It's possible to grow up in church, know Scripture, quote verses, and appear faithful on the surface, yet never have a faith that changes how we live. That kind of faith, James says, is no better than the faith of demons.

True faith shows up in everyday obedience. It's visible in how you love your wife, raise your kids, handle your money, treat people who wrong you, and walk in integrity when no one's watching. A living faith reveals God through action, not mere lip service.

So, the question James presses on us is simple but powerful: *Does your life show what your lips profess?*

Application Questions

1. How does James distinguish between true faith in God and mere head knowledge of God?
2. Why does James use demons as an example of empty faith?
3. Where in your life could your works better reflect the faith you profess?
4. How do your daily decisions provide visible evidence of your faith?

A Prayer for Your Day

Father, thank You for reminding me that real faith isn't what I say or what I know, it's how I live. I don't want to settle for a belief that stays in my head but never reaches my heart or hands. Teach me to obey You in the small, unseen moments of my life. Let my faith be alive, visible, and useful for Your Kingdom. Produce in me the kind of works that bring You glory and draw others to Your truth. Amen.

DAY 13

FAITH PERFECTED BY WORKS

"For as the body apart from the spirit is dead, so also faith apart from works is dead."
—JAMES 2:26

READ JAMES 2:21–26: James closes this section with two of the more well-known characters in all of Scripture: Abraham and Rahab. Both of these folks lived in completely different worlds; one was a patriarch and the other was a prostitute. But both of their lives revealed the same truth: real faith always shows itself through action.

If we know one thing, brother, it's that Abraham's faith wasn't theoretical. How do we know? Because when God asked him to offer Isaac, the son of promise, Abraham obeyed in a way that few fathers would. That act didn't *earn* his salvation; it *proved* it. James writes, "You see that faith was active along with his works, and faith was completed by his works" (v.22). Abraham's obedience showed that his faith was alive and mature. What he believed internally was made visible externally through trust and action.

Rahab's story tells the same truth from a very different angle. She wasn't part of God's chosen people, and her life choices certainly didn't fit the religious mold. Yet when she heard about the God of Israel, she believed. That belief led her to risk her life by hiding the Israelite spies. Her faith wasn't neat or polished, but it was *real*. It acted when it mattered most. James says her works justified her faith (v.25); they showed it to be genuine.

Through these examples, James drives his final point in this section home: "For as the body apart from the spirit is dead, so also faith apart from works is dead" (v.26). Faith that doesn't act, that doesn't obey, and that doesn't sacrifice, it's not faith at all. It's nothing but a shell.

Brother, this is a challenge for you and me. It's easy to say we trust God, but when was the last time your obedience cost you something? Never forget that faith that costs nothing is worth nothing. Living faith moves us to action, whether that's leading our families in prayer, standing firm in integrity when no one's watching, or serving others when it's inconvenient.

Abraham and Rahab remind us that real faith is never static. It always acts.

Application Questions

1. What do Abraham and Rahab teach us about the relationship between faith and works?
2. Why does James say faith is "completed" by works?
3. How might God be calling you to step out in costly obedience right now?
4. What would others see if they tried to "show" your faith by your works?

A Prayer for Your Day

Father, I don't want my faith to be empty words or good intentions. I want a faith that moves, that obeys, that trusts You even when it costs me something. Give me the courage to act when You call and to follow You in every area of my life. Let my obedience prove that my faith is alive and that my heart belongs to You. Amen.

DAY 14

THE WEIGHT OF TEACHING

"Not many of you should become teachers, my brothers, for you know that we who teach will be judged with greater strictness."
—JAMES 3:1

READ JAMES 3:1–2. James opens this chapter with a strong warning: not everyone should be a teacher. Now, this isn't meant to discourage people from sharing their faith, but to remind us of the weight that comes with handling God's Word. Teaching Scripture isn't a hobby. It's not a platform for opinions or charisma. It's a sacred responsibility.

Years ago, when I began to lean into God's calling to teach the Bible, I quickly realized that I wasn't just conveying information, I was shaping lives. (Well, more accurately, the Holy Spirit was working through me to shape lives.) It's for this reason that James says teachers will be judged more strictly. The more influence you have, the more accountable you are for how you use it. If you're going to claim to speak for God, you'd better make sure you're actually speaking for Him.

We live in a culture that values personality over truth. If someone is charismatic in their personality and has a large following, people tend to view these qualities as signs that these individuals are effective teachers. But the church can't afford to treat teaching that way. It's not about someone's following or whether they are entertaining. It's about how trustworthy they are with the word of God.

That's why humility is key. We all stumble, James says. We all fall short. The best teachers are the ones who never forget that. They approach the Word with fear and trembling, knowing they're accountable to the God who wrote it.

Brother, this truth applies even if you're not standing behind a pulpit. You might be teaching your kids, leading a small group, or mentoring someone younger in the faith. The same principle stands. Your words carry weight. Handle them carefully.

Teaching is a badge of honor and a burden of responsibility. But when we carry it with reverence and dependence on the Spirit, it becomes one of the most powerful ways to serve the Kingdom.

Application Questions

1. Why do you think James warns so strongly about becoming a teacher?
2. How can you cultivate humility and dependence on God when you lead or teach others?
3. Who in your life is influenced by your example or words, even if you're not an official "teacher"?
4. What steps can you take to ensure your teaching or influence reflects God's truth, not your own opinion?

A Prayer for Your Day

Father, I thank You for the privilege of knowing our Word. Help me treat it with reverence. Guard my heart from pride or carelessness. When I teach or lead others, help me speak with truth, humility, and love. Let my words reflect Your wisdom, not my ego. Shape me into someone who represents You well in all I say and do. Amen.

DAY 15

SMALL BUT MIGHTY

"So also the tongue is a small member, yet it boasts of great things."
— JAMES 3:5

READ JAMES 3:3–6. The tongue is one of the smallest parts of the body, but it has an enormous influence. James paints two unforgettable pictures to drive home his point: a small bit that controls a massive horse, and a tiny rudder that steers a great ship. That's a very clear visual, isn't it? You can control a thousand-pound animal with a small piece of metal. You can guide a ship across an ocean with a piece of wood the size of your arm. That's your tongue. It can steer your life toward God's glory or straight into ruin.

The tongue is the steering wheel of the heart. Wherever your words go, your life follows. That's why James warns us that "the tongue is a fire, a world of unrighteousness." It's capable of great blessing, but also of immense destruction. One careless sentence can ruin a friendship. One lie can wreck a reputation. One angry outburst can scar a child or a marriage.

Brother, what comes out of our mouths exposes what's really going on inside of us. We can play at religion, but our mouths usually tell on us. We can show up to church, sing the songs, and nod our heads in prayer, but if gossip, sarcasm, or bitterness spill out of our mouths the rest of the week, it's not our tongues that need correction; it's our hearts.

Here's the great news: When the Holy Spirit is in control, He tames the tongue. He teaches us to speak life, not death. He teaches us to flavor our words with grace instead of poison. But to latch onto the power of the Spirit, we have to put ourselves in the position, mentally and spiritually, to be led by Him.

So, the real question for every man is simple: Who's holding the reins? If Jesus has your heart, He'll eventually have your words, too. But if your speech is wild and reckless, it's time to ask who's really steering your life.

Application Questions

1. What do your words this week reveal about who's ruling your heart?
2. How can you make space each day to let the Holy Spirit filter your speech before you speak?
3. What relationship could begin to heal if you started using your words to build instead of tear down?
4. Who needs encouragement from your mouth today—and what's keeping you from saying it?

A Prayer for Your Day

Father, I know my words have power. Too often, I've used them for harm instead of healing. Forgive me for speaking without self-control. Take hold of my heart and tame my tongue. Let what I say reflect Your Spirit in me. Help me speak life, grace, and truth wherever I go. Amen

DAY 16

WHEN WORDS WOUND

"But no human being can tame the tongue.
It is a restless evil, full of deadly poison."
—JAMES 3:8

READ JAMES 3:7–12. We're continuing in our examination of how our words have power. James doesn't pull any punches here (he never really does). He calls the tongue "a restless evil." And James isn't being dramatic for effect. He's being honest. Think about it for a moment: humanity has figured out how to train wild animals, how to build machines that fly, and how to harness the power of nature, but we still can't control our own mouths.

What James is telling us here is something most of us have already discovered: You can't tame the tongue by sheer willpower alone. You can't wake up and say, "I'm just not going to lose my temper today," and expect that to last past breakfast. James makes it clear that taming the tongue is a matter of discipleship, not just discipline. Only the Holy Spirit can bridle the words that come from an unguarded heart.

Our mouths can do real damage. Maybe you've done some damage with yours before, or been on the receiving end of some damaging talk. Most of us have. James compares words to poison, because what starts small can spread and infect everything it touches. Words spoken in anger, sarcasm, or arrogance have a way of staying lodged in someone's memory long after we've forgotten that we ever said them. We can bless God one minute and curse people made in His image the next. James says, "My brothers, these things ought not to be so."

There is a great inconsistency in our Christian living, one that has bothered me for some time. The inconsistency comes in the words of many men who claim to follow Christ. They profess faith in Jesus, but their words don't align with their actions. How many men do you know that sing worship songs on Sunday with the same mouth they use to gossip or tear somebody down all week long? If both praise and profanity are being drawn out of us, we've got something wrong with the well. James echoes that: fresh water and salt water don't flow from the same spring.

Christian, the tongue doesn't need managing. The tongue needs transforming. If you want to change what comes out of your mouth, let God change what's inside your heart. When the Spirit rules there, your words begin to sound a lot more like Jesus.

Application Questions

1. Why do you think James calls the tongue a "restless evil"?
2. In what situations are you most likely to speak words you regret?
3. How could inviting the Holy Spirit to rule your speech change your relationships?
4. Who needs to hear confession or forgiveness from your mouth this week?

A Prayer for Your Day

Father, I confess that my words have too often been careless and harmful. I can't tame my tongue on my own. I need Your Spirit to change my heart so that what comes out of my mouth reflects Your grace. Teach me to speak truth, love, and encouragement, and to bring life where my words once caused harm. Amen.

DAY 17

WISDOM FROM ABOVE

"Who is wise and understanding among you? By his good conduct let him show his works in the meekness of wisdom."
— JAMES 3:13

READ JAMES 3:13–18. James transitions from his discussion of the power of our words to the power of our thoughts. James spends the final verses of chapter three talking about wisdom. It's a fitting subject after such a powerful treatment of our words and how we use them.

You can talk about how smart you are all day long, but if it doesn't show up in how you live, you don't have wisdom; you only have information. That's the heartbeat of James 3:13–18. James distinguishes between two kinds of wisdom: one that comes from the world and one that comes from above.

Worldly wisdom is loud and proud. It's often self-promoting. It's the kind that says, "Look at me. Look what I know. Look what I've done." Usually, it's driven by ego and selfish ambition. James says that kind of wisdom doesn't come from God. It *can't* come from God. That kind of wisdom is worldly and unspiritual. If your so-called wisdom makes you arrogant, then you've got the wrong source. That's not wisdom from heaven. That's not godly wisdom.

True wisdom, the kind that comes from above, looks like Jesus. It's pure, peaceable, gentle, open to reason, full of mercy, and bears good fruit. It's not about being the loudest man in the room; it's about being the godliest. It's not wisdom that's demonstrated in how clever you are; it's wisdom that is shown in how you treat people. You don't prove you're wise by winning arguments. You prove it by the way you live your life.

Brother, we live in a culture that celebrates cleverness but rarely honors character. The world will tell you to chase success, power, and status. But James says that godly wisdom is evident in humility and peace. The truly wise man isn't looking to win every fight. Instead, he is looking to please God.

James closes by saying, "A harvest of righteousness is sown in peace by those who make peace." In other words, godly wisdom produces godly fruit. If your decisions, your conversations, and your leadership lead to peace and righteousness, you're walking in wisdom from above.

Application Questions

1. What's the difference between worldly wisdom and godly wisdom in your own life?
2. How can you tell whether your decisions are being driven by pride or by peace?
3. What would change in your home, work, or church if you sought wisdom from above first?
4. Where do you most need God's wisdom right now?

A Prayer for Your Day

Father, I don't want to settle for the world's version of wisdom. It's loud and empty. Give me wisdom from above, wisdom that is pure, humble, and full of peace. Help me live it out in how I speak, lead, and love. Teach me to sow peace and reap righteousness for Your glory. Amen.

DAY 18

THE REAL SOURCE OF OUR CONFLICTS

"What causes quarrels and what causes fights among you? Is it not this, that your passions are at war within you? You desire and do not have, so you murder. You covet and cannot obtain, so you fight and quarrel. You do not have, because you do not ask. You ask and do not receive, because you ask wrongly, to spend it on your passions."
—JAMES 4:1–3

READ JAMES 4:1–3. James doesn't waste words. He goes straight for the heart. In these verses, he exposes a truth most of us would rather ignore: the problem isn't "out there," it's "in here." Every conflict, every broken relationship, and every moral failure begins in our hearts. Before the brokenness of sin spills into our homes, workplaces, or churches, it starts within us.

James pulls back the curtain and reveals what's truly driving that war: our desires. The Greek word for "passions" (*hēdonē*) is where we get the word *hedonism*, which means "the pursuit of pleasure." It's living for self, chasing whatever makes us feel good or look good in the moment. Our desires for control, comfort, or recognition often take the throne that belongs to Christ.

When you make your feelings your god, you'll always end up in conflict. Think about that. Most of the time, the tension we feel with others isn't just about them. The tension often arises from our craving for something we believe we deserve. Maybe it's respect we want. Or perhaps it's comfort, or even a sense of control. But when we chase those desires, not only are we chasing things that the Lord doesn't want us to chase, we often begin to view other Christ-followers as competitors instead of brothers.

What James does next is pretty powerful: he connects the war in our hearts to our prayer lives. He says, "You do not have because you do not ask." And when we *do* ask, we often "ask wrongly," wanting God to bless our own agenda.

A lot of us aren't praying for God's will to be done; we're praying for our will to be done and asking God to rubber-stamp it. That's a hard truth, brother, but an important one.

Never forget this: prayer isn't about convincing God to give us what we want; it's about aligning our hearts with what He wants. When our prayers are shaped by our selfish motives, they lose their power. But when we pray in surrender, asking God to reshape our desires to align with His will, God's peace begins to take root within us. That has been true in my life, and if you have walked with God for any length of time, I know it has been true for you, as well.

If there's a battle raging inside you today (anger, envy, frustration, discontent, etc.), don't look for someone else to blame. Look inward. The peace you long for in your home, your relationships, and your heart starts when you surrender your desires to Christ.

When you want what He wants, the war within begins to quiet down.

Application Questions

1. Where do you most feel the "war within" right now: home, work, or relationships? Who has been hurt by your selfish desires that you need to ask forgiveness?
2. How can selfish desires subtly drive your prayers and decisions?
3. What would it look like to surrender your motives completely to Christ this week?
4. How might unity among believers grow if we each started fighting sin instead of each other?

A Prayer for Your Day

Lord, help me see the battles raging in my own heart. Teach me to want what You want. I confess that too often my prayers and my choices come from selfish desires. Quiet the war within me, and make me a man of peace who lives by Your will, not mine. Amen.

DAY 19

SPIRITUAL INFIDELITY

"You adulterous people! Do you not know that friendship with the world is enmity with God? Therefore whoever wishes to be a friend of the world makes himself an enemy of God."
—JAMES 4:4

READ JAMES 4:4–5. James does not ease into this passage or soften his words. He speaks like a man who loves the church too much to lie to her. When he uses the word *adulterous*, he is saying something every man needs to hear clearly: divided loyalty to God is betrayal. Friendship with the world will always place a man in conflict with the Lord. There is no safe way to chase the world while claiming devotion to Christ.

James is writing to the church, not the lost. He is confronting people who consider themselves believers and warning them that living under the world's system makes them unfaithful to their Groom. Scripture has always spoken this way. God does not describe His people as customers or coworkers. He calls them His bride. And when His bride runs after other lovers like success, comfort, approval, and control, He describes it for what it is: unfaithfulness.

Anywhere in your life where spiritually you are not fully committed to Jesus, you are committing spiritual adultery. This is not about outward religion. It is about affection. It is about what you depend on when pressure hits. It is about what excites you, comforts you, and drives your decisions. A man can attend church, carry a Bible, even pray, and still be more loyal to the world than to Christ.

Then James reveals something staggering about God's heart: "He yearns jealously over the spirit that He has made to dwell in us." God is not distant about your devotion. He is not detached. He does not watch your divided heart without response. He yearns for you with covenant love. God does not share His bride. He will not negotiate your allegiance.

This kind of unfaithful living invites divine displeasure. God resists pride. He does not silently accept divided loyalty. Friendship with the world produces spiritual hostility toward God, whether a man realizes it or not.

So, brother, ask yourself honestly: Where has my loyalty shifted? What do I defend that Scripture confronts? What behaviors have I normalized that God calls sin? What am I chasing that competes with obedience?

God is not looking for part of your heart. He is a Husband. And He does not accept shared devotion. James is calling you out because God is calling you back.

Application Questions

1. Where has your loyalty quietly shifted? Where has devotion to the world diluted devotion to Christ?
2. What have you normalized that Scripture confronts? Are there habits, attitudes, or compromises you excuse that God's Word clearly exposes?
3. What would repentance actually look like in your life this week? Identify one concrete step of obedience that represents returning your loyalty to Christ.

A Prayer for Your Day

Lord, You see where my loyalty has drifted and where my heart has chased the wrong things. I confess the ways I have divided my affection and trusted the world more than You. Turn my heart back to You and give me a greater love for what honors You. Thank You for calling me back instead of letting me wander. Amen.

DAY 20

GRACE FOR THE HUMBLE

"You adulterous people! Do you not know that friendship with the world is enmity with God? Therefore whoever wishes to be a friend of the world makes himself an enemy of God."

—JAMES 4:4

READ JAMES 4:4–6. James is nothing if not straightforward, a fact you have discovered by now. He calls believers "adulterous people," not because they've been unfaithful to a spouse, but because they've been unfaithful to God. The people James was talking about were being spiritually adulterous. You see, we cheat on God every time we give our loyalty, our affection, or our devotion to the world instead of Him. That's what spiritual adultery is: loving the world's ways more than God's.

The "world" James speaks of isn't creation itself. When the Bible talks about "the world," it's the system of values and priorities that stand in opposition to God, that govern our society. It's the mindset that chases power, pleasure, and comfort instead of holiness, humility, and obedience. And as Christians, we're called to live differently from the world.

If we have been redeemed by faith in Jesus, we can't live like the world all week and act like we love Jesus on Sunday. The world calls us to self: self-promotion, self-preservation, self-gratification, and so on. The Gospel calls us to surrender. And here, James is reminding us that there's no middle ground. Friendship with the world makes us enemies of God, not because God stops loving us, but because we've chosen to align ourselves with a kingdom that opposes His.

That may sound harsh, but it's also deeply personal. God isn't careless or "ho-hum" when His people wander. James quotes Scripture when he says that God yearns jealously over the spirit He has made to dwell in us. Now, unlike ours, God's jealousy isn't petty or insecure. Like all of His characteristics, His jealousy is holy and pure. It's the passion of a Father who refuses to share His children's hearts with false gods that can never satisfy them. His jealousy flows from love, not control. He knows that only in Him will we find joy, peace, and purpose.

And that's where the passage turns from confrontation to comfort: "But he gives more grace." Those four words are the heartbeat of hope. God's response to our unfaithfulness isn't abandonment. His response to us is grace. When you realize you've been chasing the wrong things, God doesn't write you off; He gives you more grace to come home.

That grace is the dividing line between pride and humility. God resists the proud, the man who insists he can love both the world and God, but He gives grace to the humble. The humble man is the man who finally bows low and says, "Lord, I've been running after the wrong things."

Brother, we can't love the world and love God at the same time. A divided heart will always drift toward compromise. But the man who humbles himself before God finds something far better than the world could ever offer: grace upon grace from the one who never stops pursuing His people.

Application Questions

1. What does "friendship with the world" look like in your own life? What are some areas you have drifted into comfort with the world?
2. How do you see spiritual compromise creeping into your habits or priorities?
3. Where have you experienced God's righteous jealousy, not to harm you, but to draw you back to Him?
4. How can you cultivate humility so that you receive more of His grace this week?

A Prayer for Your Day

Father, forgive me for the ways I've chased after the world instead of You. I don't want to be divided in heart or purpose. Teach me to love You with undivided devotion. Give me the humility to turn from pride and the grace to live fully for You. Amen.

DAY 21

THE PATH OF REPENTANCE

"Submit yourselves therefore to God. Resist the devil, and he will flee from you."
—JAMES 4:7

READ JAMES 4:7–10. You cannot follow Jesus halfway and expect to have victory over sin. You're either under His authority or you're not. That's what James is getting at in these verses. Spiritual victory begins with surrender. Ultimately, you don't resist the devil solely through self-help, willpower, or toughness. You resist him by submitting to the authority of God.

Submission is a word that men don't like. It feels weak. But in the Kingdom of God, submission is strength. Do you want to be a strong man? Then get on your knees. That's where the power is. When we bow our lives before God, when we surrender to Him our decisions, our thoughts, and our desires, we're no longer standing alone in the fight. We're standing under God's protection and with His power.

Then James gives a promise: "Resist the devil, and he will flee from you." Notice the order: submission comes before resistance. You can't tell Satan to leave if you're still giving him a seat at the table. But when your life is surrendered to Christ, the devil has no authority to stand.

James says, "Draw near to God, and He will draw near to you." That's one of the most incredible promises in Scripture. The God who spoke the universe into being draws near to anyone humble enough to seek Him. And it's important to remember that God doesn't usually play hard to get. If there's distance between you and Him, guess who moved?

James ends this section with a call to repentance: "Cleanse your hands . . . purify your hearts . . . humble yourselves before the Lord." Again, we see that God's Word promises to lift up the man who bows low.

Brother, we live in a world that celebrates defiance and mocks humility. But the strongest man you can ever be is a man who lives fully surrendered to Christ: submitted, resisting evil, and walking daily in His presence.

Application Questions

1. What areas of your life do you still resist submitting fully to God?
2. How have you tried to "resist the devil" in your own strength?
3. What does it look like, practically, for you to draw near to God each day?
4. How might humility actually be the most courageous thing you could practice this week?

A Prayer for Your Day

Father, I submit my life to You. I've tried too long to fight my battles alone. Teach me what it means to live under Your authority and to resist evil through Your strength. Draw near to me as I draw near to You. Cleanse my heart, humble my spirit, and make my life a reflection of Your grace. Amen.

DAY 22

HOW WE SPEAK AND HOW WE JUDGE

"Do not speak evil against one another, brothers. The one who speaks against a brother or judges his brother, speaks evil against the law and judges the law. But if you judge the law, you are not a doer of the law but a judge. There is only one lawgiver and judge, he who is able to save and to destroy. But who are you to judge your neighbor?"
— JAMES 4:11–12

READ JAMES 4:11–12. Here, James is not addressing casual gossip or careless talk; he's confronting a deeper issue: the heart behind our words. If you have a mouth problem, you probably have a heart problem. The way we talk about people, especially our brothers and sisters in Christ, reveals what's really going on inside us. When we tear others down, not only do we break a social rule, but we also break God's law of love.

James reminds us that our words are never neutral. They either build up or tear down. When we criticize, slander, or gossip, we aren't simply venting; we're assuming a position of superiority. That's why James says that when we judge others, we place ourselves above the law. That's a heavy statement.

When we act like the judge, we've forgotten that we're the ones who are supposed to be standing before the Judge. God alone has the authority to determine right and wrong, guilt and innocence. When we take that seat, we step into a role that doesn't belong to us.

There's a crucial difference between discernment and condemnation. Scripture calls us to discern truth, to recognize sin, and to call it what it is, but never to condemn another person. Condemnation belongs to God alone. There's a big difference between helping a brother out of sin and talking about him behind his back. One is motivated by love; the other by pride. Judging others harshly is a sign that we've forgotten the grace that God showed us in

Jesus. None of us earned God's mercy: it was given freely. And if we've received that kind of grace, how can we withhold it from others?

James closes with a powerful reminder: "There is only one lawgiver and judge, he who is able to save and to destroy." God alone has the right to judge because He alone has the power to save. Every time we speak evil of someone or pass judgment, we're trying to sit in His chair. That's dangerous ground for any man who's been saved by grace.

If you're spending your time judging people, you're not spending your time loving people. The call of Christ is simple but costly: extend the same mercy you've received. Brother, let's be men who build up instead of tear down, who speak life instead of condemnation, and who leave the judging to the only one who's worthy of the chair.

Application Questions

1. When are you most tempted to speak critically of others?
2. How can you tell when discernment turns into judgment?
3. What would it look like for you to speak grace instead of criticism this week?
4. How does remembering God as the ultimate Judge change how you view others?

A Prayer for Your Day

Lord, forgive me for the times I've spoken against others or acted like the judge instead of the servant. Remind me of the grace You've shown me so that I can show that same grace to others. Guard my mouth and my heart, and help me build up, not tear down. Amen.

DAY 23

THE ILLUSION OF CONTROL

"Come now, you who say, 'Today or tomorrow we will go into such and such a town and spend a year there and trade and make a profit'—yet you do not know what tomorrow will bring. What is your life? For you are a mist that appears for a little time and then vanishes."

— JAMES 4:13–14

READ JAMES 4:13–17. James ends this section of his letter with a gut check about pride and perspective. He confronts the mindset that says, *"I'm in control of my life."* Man plans, but God decides, and we'd better remember who's running the show. James is referring to individuals who make grand plans for the future (career moves, business deals, and even life goals) without consulting God. When they do this, they're scheduling their lives as if they own the clock.

We don't have a planning problem. We have a pride problem. Scripture never condemns wise preparation, but it does condemn arrogance. The issue isn't having a calendar; it's assuming tomorrow is guaranteed. We live as if we have unlimited time, but James says we're a mist, a vapor. We're here, then we're gone. That image should sober us. Life is short, fragile, and unpredictable. Every breath we take is a borrowed gift from the Lord. When we live like we're the authors of our own story, we forget who truly holds the power.

Instead of saying, "Here's what I'll do," James tells us to say, "If the Lord wills." That phrase isn't mere superstition. Instead, it's a posture of humility. It's a way of acknowledging God's sovereignty over every detail of our lives. It reminds us that He's not a consultant to our plans; He's the King who directs them. If you're living life without factoring God into your plans, that's arrogance. That's the heart of what James calls "evil boasting," living as though our will and wisdom can guarantee an outcome.

When we think that way, we rob God of the glory He deserves and set ourselves up for disappointment. Pride leads to frustration because it puts us at the center of a world that doesn't revolve around us. But humility leads to peace because it puts God back where He belongs: on the throne of our hearts.

Then James ends with one more truth that cuts deep: "Whoever knows the right thing to do and fails to do it, for him it is sin." This is a moral failure, sure, but it's also pure spiritual negligence. God's will isn't always about the next big decision. Often it's about simple obedience in the present. You don't need to know everything about tomorrow; you just need to walk faithfully in what God has shown you today.

Brother, tomorrow belongs to God. So live today with humility, obedience, and gratitude because today might be all you get.

Application Questions

1. When do you tend to plan or act as if you're in control instead of God?
2. How would your daily attitude change if you truly believed "if the Lord wills"?
3. What's one area of your life where you need to surrender your plans to God?
4. Why do you think James calls boasting about the future "evil"?

A Prayer for Your Day

Lord, teach me to number my days and live each one for You. Keep me from pride that forgets who's in control. Help me make plans with humility, always holding them open before You. My life is Yours. Guide my steps today and every day, if it be Your will. Amen.

DAY 24

A BETTER WAY TO PLAN

"Instead you ought to say,
'If the Lord wills, we will live and do this or that.'"
—JAMES 4:15

READ JAMES 4:15. Here, James says, "If the Lord wills, we will live and do this or that." That one sentence has a way of wrecking a man's sense of control, doesn't it? We talk about next week, next year, five-year plans, and retirement as if we owned tomorrow. James comes along and reminds us that every breath is borrowed.

The most arrogant thing we can do is act like we are guaranteed another day. You can make outlines, build calendars, and set goals, but when a man talks like he controls his future, his life is already showing who he answers to. There is nothing wrong with planning. The issue is our attitude. Planning reveals what a man believes about authority.

As God has continued to sanctify me, my language has changed over time. Instead of me saying, "We'll see you tomorrow," you might hear me say, "We'll see you tomorrow, Lord willing." That change isn't just religious talk; it's a spiritual reset. It's a daily reminder that God decides whether tomorrow even exists. When we speak that way, we are declaring our dependence.

James drives it home by asking, "What is your life?" Then he answers, "You are a mist that appears for a little time and then vanishes." This hit me the hardest when I stood at my son Bronner's graveside and realized how certain I once felt about the future. I thought I knew how things would go. I thought I had time. Then reality showed me who actually holds the calendar.

When I was standing on a baseball field, thinking about how my son would never get to play in a Little League game, God whispered a hard truth into my heart: The length of a life does not determine its completeness. Every day is already written. God never miscalculates time. A man may think something ended early, but heaven calls it right on schedule.

When a man says, "If the Lord wills," he is doing more than acknowledging God. He is surrendering control. He is accepting that God shapes outcomes. He is trusting that blessings withheld are as intentional as blessings given. God has saved you from things you never even knew were coming.

James is calling men to walk with open hands. Make plans. Dream boldly. Work hard. Then lay it all before God and trust Him to hold the future better than you ever could.

Faithful men build their lives with humility. And humility leaves room for God to rule what you cannot.

"If the Lord wills." That is how a man who knows God steps into tomorrow.

Application Questions

1. Where are you speaking about the future as if the outcome is already decided?
2. What plan or goal do you need to place entirely into God's hands right now?
3. How could your language better reflect trust in the Lord's control this week?

A Prayer for Your Day

Lord, I confess that I often speak and plan as if tomorrow were guaranteed. Teach me to live with humility and to trust You with my future. Help me to hold every plan with open hands and a surrendered heart. I want my life to reflect dependence on You in every decision I make. Amen.

DAY 25

THE SIN OF KNOWING AND NOT DOING

"As it is, you boast in your arrogance. All such boasting is evil. So whoever knows the right thing to do and fails to do it, for him it is sin."
—JAMES 4:16–17

READ JAMES 4:16–17. James closes the chapter with a sentence that leaves no wiggle room: "So whoever knows the right thing to do and fails to do it, for him it is sin." That line stands like a verdict. A man either responds or walks away unchanged.

At this point, James moves from ideas to accountability. Earlier, he had dealt with pride, planning, and presumption. Here, he brings everything down to one question: What will you actually do with what God has already shown you? This is where Christianity steps from information into obedience.

I have long called this area "sins of omission." These are the moments when a man clearly understands God's will and chooses to delay. He knows to forgive, yet holds onto the wound. He knows how to lead his family, yet chooses to be passive. He knows he should confess, yet he protects his image. God has provided clarity. The man offers excuses.

Here me, brother: Repeated exposure without response hardens the heart. A man can attend church for years, hear strong teaching, feel occasional conviction, and then push it aside. Over time, the edge comes off the truth. Messages feel familiar. Conviction grows softer. Eventually, the Word feels like background noise rather than marching orders.

James refuses to let that pattern feel safe. He ties sin directly to ignored obedience. A man who knows the right thing and chooses comfort steps into rebellion with full awareness. That choice may feel small in the moment. Over time, those small choices shape a life story.

Years ago, God showed me that heaven does not treat these decisions as minor. God never reveals a step of obedience by accident. When He puts His finger on an area of your life, He is inviting change. That invitation carries grace and responsibility. God supplies the strength to move, and He also expects movement.

So this passage presses in with a simple question: what has God already told you to do? You may think of a conversation you need to have, a habit you need to lay down, a step of leadership you keep postponing, or a private sin you keep hiding. The Holy Spirit brings those things to mind on purpose.

James will not let men hide behind vague spirituality. Genuine faith walks into obedience while there is still time to respond. God speaks. You understand. Heaven waits to see what you do next.

Application Questions

1. What has God already told you to do that you have been putting off?
2. Where have you grown comfortable with delay instead of obedience?
3. What one step of action represented faithfulness for you this week?

A Prayer for Your Day

Lord, You have made Your will clearer than I often want to admit. Forgive me for the times I have delayed what You have already shown me. Give me the courage to obey and the humility to respond quickly. Help me walk faithfully in the places You continue to press on my heart. Amen.

DAY 26

WHEN WEALTH CORRUPTS

"You have lived on the earth in luxury and in self-indulgence. You have fattened your hearts in a day of slaughter. You have condemned and murdered the righteous person. He does not resist you."
— JAMES 5:5–6

READ JAMES 5:1–6. These verses are among the most direct and unsettling passages in James' letter, and for good reason. James doesn't condemn wealth itself; he's confronting the heart behind it. James is helping us see a powerful truth: if our goal is to be comfortable, to make life all about us, then our wealth is a false idol that's rotting us from the inside out. Money isn't evil, but making it your god is. The issue isn't what's in your bank account; it's what's ruling your heart.

James paints a haunting picture. He says the rich who hoard and exploit others have treasures that are "rotted," garments that are "moth-eaten," and gold that's "corroded." He's showing that anything we build apart from God eventually decays. We can spend our whole lives chasing money, but one day, we'll leave it all behind. The question is, what have we done with our resources while we were here? Because there are only really two choices: we'll either use our money for the Kingdom, or it will testify against us before God. The things we cling to in this life will either become tools for God's glory or evidence of our misplaced trust.

The people James rebukes were both selfish and unjust. They gained wealth by cheating workers. They padded their comfort with the suffering of others, and James says that their cries reached "the ears of the Lord of hosts." Brother, you might fool the world, but you won't fool the Lord of Hosts. God sees every act of greed and every moment of generosity. He takes injustice personally because He values people, not possessions.

This passage applies to us as well as the ancient rich people James was originally writing to. Every man is storing up something. We're either investing in eternity or hoarding for ourselves. The question isn't whether we'll leave it all behind; it's what legacy we'll leave when we do. Guess what? Comfort fades and wealth rusts. But a man who uses what God's given him for God's purposes stores up treasure that will never corrode.

Don't let what you own end up owning you. That's the warning and the invitation from this passage. Wealth can be a blessing or a trap, depending on whether we view our resources as our own or as God's. God gives to each what He will give, not to make us more comfortable but to make us more effective. The antidote to greed isn't guilt, it's generosity. When you live openhanded before God, money loses its grip on your heart.

So, before you chase what's next, stop and ask: What story is your spending, saving, and giving telling about who your God really is?

Application Questions

1. What's the difference between having wealth and being owned by it?
2. How can success or comfort quietly replace your dependence on God?
3. Who might God be calling you to bless or make right with financially or relationally?
4. How does generosity serve as protection against greed?

A Prayer for Your Day

Father, thank You for every blessing You've entrusted me with. Guard my heart from greed, pride, or self-reliance. Teach me to use my resources to build Your Kingdom and not my own comfort. Help me live with open hands, grateful hearts, and eyes fixed on what truly lasts. Amen.

DAY 27

BE PATIENT FOR THE HARVEST

"Be patient, therefore, brothers, until the coming of the Lord. See how the farmer waits for the precious fruit of the earth, being patient about it, until it receives the early and the late rains. You also, be patient. Establish your hearts, for the coming of the Lord is at hand."

— JAMES 5:7–8

READ JAMES 5:7–8. Here, James provides one of the clearest pictures of what faithful endurance looks like: that of the farmer. A farmer can't rush the harvest. He can't make it rain when he wants, and he can't speed up the growth of the seed. The farmer can't manipulate the sun. All he can do is work faithfully and wait patiently. That's the picture of Christian perseverance. Like the farmer, we are to be steady, doing grounded work while trusting God with what only He can control.

Patience in Scripture doesn't mean doing nothing. Being patient is a sign of resilience. Biblical patience is active trust. It's continuing to do what's right, even when the results are invisible. Waiting on God doesn't mean you stop moving. It means you keep walking in obedience even when you can't see the results yet. That's hard for most men because we live in a world that worships speed and control. However, spiritual maturity often involves learning to wait faithfully when you'd rather force a solution.

James uses the phrase "establish your hearts," meaning to strengthen or anchor your inner life, to stand firm when everything around you feels uncertain. The man who's grounded in Christ doesn't come apart when life gets hard. He's got roots. He's steady because he knows who's in control. The farmer doesn't panic when rain delays the season. He's seen dry spells before. Experience has taught him that growth takes time. Likewise, the longer you walk with Christ, the more you learn to trust His timing.

James connects this endurance to the return of Jesus. The waiting isn't pointless. The waiting is preparation. Every trial, delay, and frustration is shaping us to look more like Christ. The problem with most men today is that we want instant results in a microwave world. But God grows things in seasons, not seconds. There's no shortcut to spiritual maturity. Growth happens in the quiet, hidden places where faith is tested and refined.

So, brother, keep plowing. Keep praying. Keep trusting. Don't give up just because the fruit hasn't shown up yet. God always delivers on His promises, but He does it on His timeline, not ours. Like a farmer who trusts that the harvest will come when the season is ready, we trust that God's timing is perfect and His purposes never fail.

Endurance isn't glamorous, but it's the soil where real faith grows. Hold steady and stay faithful. Do the work of patience. The harvest will come. We just have to hold our ground until it does.

Application Questions

1. What are you currently waiting for God to do?
2. How can you actively practice patience instead of frustration?
3. What would it look like to "establish your heart" in this season?
4. How has God used waiting to strengthen your faith in the past?

A Prayer for Your Day

Lord, help me wait well. Teach me to trust Your timing instead of demanding my own. Strengthen my heart when I get restless or weary, and remind me that You never waste a season. Grow my faith while I wait for the harvest You've promised. Amen.

DAY 28

PERSEVERING THROUGH SUFFERING

"Behold, we consider those blessed who remained steadfast. You have heard of the steadfastness of Job, and you have seen the purpose of the Lord, how the Lord is compassionate and merciful."
—JAMES 5:11

JAMES 5:9–11 REMINDS US that suffering and patience aren't opposites; they're companions. God is not hiding the ball from us. He's straight up about it. The Christian life will inevitably include hardship. Following Jesus doesn't mean avoiding difficulty; it means trusting Him through it. If you're walking with Christ, you're walking against the current of the world, and that current pushes back.

James calls believers to persevere like Job, who suffered more than most of us could imagine. Job lost everything: his wealth, his health, his children, and even the encouragement of his own wife. Yet in all of it, he refused to curse God. Job wasn't perfect, but he stayed in the fight. He didn't understand what God was doing, but he didn't walk away either. That's the essence of biblical perseverance: faith that clings to God when every emotion, circumstance, and voice around you says, "Give up."

A lot of us want to be mighty men of faith, but we don't want to go through what mighty men went through to become that way. Strength doesn't come from ease; it's forged in adversity. God doesn't waste suffering. He uses trials to refine us, to scrape away pride, and to produce endurance. Every season of struggle is an opportunity to learn dependence, humility, and hope.

Suffering is not a sign of God's absence. It's often the most unmistakable evidence of His presence and purpose. Job emerged from his trial with a deeper faith and a more accurate understanding of God's character. His story reminds us that endurance is about trusting the heart of the one who's in control, not just gritting your teeth and buckling down. God doesn't call us to endure alone. God always walks with us through the pain.

James also warns believers not to grumble against one another. When life hurts, frustration often spills over to the people closest to us. But bitterness and complaining erode the very faith suffering is meant to build. We can't claim to trust God and then take it out on our brothers when things get rough.

So, when life presses in, resist the urge to complain or quit. Instead, stay in the fight. Keep your eyes on the Lord, who is compassionate, merciful, and faithful to the end. You may not see the whole picture now, but one day, like Job, you'll look back and realize that every tear and trial was preparing you for something greater.

Application Questions

1. How do you typically respond when life gets hard—faith or frustration?
2. What lessons have you learned from past seasons of suffering?
3. Why is patience such an essential part of spiritual maturity?
4. How can remembering God's mercy reshape how you handle hardship?

A Prayer for Your Day

Father, help me endure the hard seasons without losing sight of Your goodness. When I grow weary, remind me that You are compassionate and merciful. Strengthen my heart to trust You when I can't see what You're doing. Help me suffer well, with patience and faith. Amen.

DAY 29

THE POWER OF INTEGRITY

"But above all, my brothers, do not swear,
either by heaven or by earth or by any other oath,
but let your 'yes' be yes and your 'no' be no,
so that you may not fall under condemnation."
—JAMES 5:12

READ JAMES 5:12. This verse may seem like a sudden shift, but it lands like a hammer. After warning about pride, impatience, and careless words, James zeroes in on something deeply practical: integrity. For the Christian man in today's world, integrity matters more than just about any other trait. We must be men of integrity.

In the first century, people often tried to prove their sincerity by swearing on something greater than themselves. They'd swear on heaven, earth, or even God's name. It was a way of saying, "I really mean it this time." But James echoes Jesus' words in Matthew 5:37: "Let your 'yes' be yes and your 'no' be no." The message is simple but convicting. Why? Because truth doesn't need backup. When your life is marked by honesty, you don't need to add flair or drama. People learn that your word stands on its own. If you have to swear to make people believe you, that's a character problem. A man whose word carries no weight has a spiritual problem long before he has a credibility one.

Here's a powerful truth I learned a long time ago: You don't have to convince anybody with talk; just be consistent. Over time, your life will speak for itself. That's integrity. It's doing what you said you'd do, especially when it costs you. It's showing up when you said you would, telling the truth when it's inconvenient, and following through even when nobody's watching. The world is full of men who overpromise and underdeliver. The man of God flips that pattern. The man of God promises little (i.e., carefully and judiciously) and delivers much.

James warns that without integrity, we "fall under condemnation." That's not because we occasionally stumble over words, but because habitual dishonesty reveals a divided heart. A man who manipulates truth to get his way or to save face damages relationships and his witness. If you say you belong to Jesus, but your word can't be trusted, why would anybody take your faith seriously? The world doesn't need more talk. The world needs men whose lives are stable, steady, and trustworthy.

Integrity is the backbone of leadership. Whether it's at home, at work, or in the church, credibility is earned through consistency. When you tell your wife you'll handle something, handle it. When you promise your kids you'll show up, make sure to do so. When you commit to a brother in Christ, keep that commitment.

A man whose "yes" means yes and whose "no" means no doesn't need to advertise his character. His consistency speaks louder than any oath ever could. Real integrity isn't built in a moment. Real integrity, the kind that lasts, is forged through thousands of small choices to tell the truth and keep your word.

Application Questions

1. How consistent is your word—do people know they can depend on it?
2. Why does honesty carry so much weight in your witness?
3. Where might you need to restore integrity in your commitments?
4. How can your "yes" and "no" reflect the truth of Christ in you?

A Prayer for Your Day

Lord, make me a man of integrity. Help my words and actions align so that people see Your truth in how I live. Teach me to be dependable, honest, and steady in all things. May my yes mean yes, my no mean no, and my life point others to You. Amen.

DAY 30

THE POWER OF PRAYER

"Is anyone among you suffering? Let him pray. Is anyone cheerful? Let him sing praise. Is anyone among you sick? Let him call for the elders of the church, and let them pray over him, anointing him with oil in the name of the Lord. And the prayer of faith will save the one who is sick, and the Lord will raise him up. And if he has committed sins, he will be forgiven."

—JAMES 5:13–15

READ JAMES 5:13–18. This is one of the most practical passages in the whole letter. It shows us what to do in every season of life: pray. James says if you're suffering, pray. If you're cheerful, sing praises. If you're sick, call the elders to pray. In other words, no matter where you find yourself (whether in pain, joy, or uncertainty), the correct response is always turning toward God. The problem with most of us is that prayer is often our last resort, rather than our first response. We'll call a friend, complain to a coworker, or try to fix it ourselves before we ever hit our knees. But James reminds us that prayer isn't an emergency lever; it's a lifeline.

Real men pray. Not just before meals or when the bottom drops out, but daily, intentionally, and persistently. Prayer is about a relationship, not about checking a religious box. It's where we bring our hearts before God and let Him align our will with His. It's where strength replaces anxiety. It's where faith grows through dependence. To experience the power of God in your life, you must remain connected to the source. Prayer isn't optional.

James talks about personal prayer but also points to the power of community. "Let him call for the elders," he says. There's wisdom in inviting others into your struggle. We're not meant to fight alone. When you're hurting, you need brothers who will cover you in prayer and remind you that you're not alone and that you're not forgotten. God designed His church to be a place where prayer brings healing and faith produces restoration. Men who pray together become men who stand together.

Then James gives us the example of Elijah. Elijah wasn't superhuman; he just believed that God meant what He said. The only difference between Elijah's prayers and ours is that Elijah actually believed God would do what He promised. That's faith. It's not confidence in the size of our prayer, it's confidence in the character of our God.

Prayer changes our circumstances. But it also change us. It shapes our hearts, deepens our trust, and reminds us that we serve a God who hears. So, brother, whatever season you're in, make prayer your first move, not your last resort. When life is good, give thanks. When it's hard, cry out. When it's uncertain, stand firm in faith.

Your situation does not limit God's power. No matter where you find yourself, God still answers, still heals, and still restores.

Application Questions

1. How often do you turn to prayer as your *first* response instead of your last?
2. Who are the people you can count on to pray with and for you?
3. What would change in your life if you prayed with Elijah-like confidence?
4. How has God used prayer to strengthen or redirect you in hard times?

A Prayer for Your Day

Father, forgive me for treating prayer like an emergency exit instead of a daily lifeline. Teach me to pray with faith, persistence, and confidence in Your power. Help me depend on You first, not myself. Strengthen my heart to believe that You still move through the prayers of Your people. Amen.

DAY 31

RESTORING THE WANDERING BROTHER

"My brothers, if anyone among you wanders from the truth and someone brings him back, let him know that whoever brings back a sinner from his wandering will save his soul from death and will cover a multitude of sins."
— JAMES 5:19–20

READ JAMES 5:19–20. James closes his letter not with a soft goodbye but with a charge. "My brothers," he says, "if anyone among you wanders from the truth and someone brings him back, let him know that whoever brings back a sinner from his wandering will save his soul from death and cover a multitude of sins." It's a fitting conclusion to a letter that's been all about living faith. James doesn't end with theory but with a mission.

If you know a man who's drifting, and you do nothing, you're not loving him, you're abandoning him. This is where faith becomes action. Genuine faith doesn't stand by when a brother stumbles. It steps in. The call to go after a wandering brother is a command, not an option. Stepping in when people are floundering is what the church looks like when it's healthy. When a man drifts from God (whether into sin, cynicism, or spiritual apathy), the men around him have a responsibility to pursue him. Restoration isn't comfortable work, but it's Gospel work.

James makes it clear: the stakes are eternal. "Whoever brings back a sinner from his wandering will save his soul from death." That's heavy. Every man you know is heading toward one of two outcomes: life or death. And God often uses other believers as His rescue plan. The world's version of love says, "Let people do what makes them happy." God's version says, "Go get them before sin destroys them." Love doesn't look the other way; it steps into the mess with courage and grace.

Too many men choose isolation over engagement. We see somebody slipping and we tell ourselves, “That’s none of my business.” But if you belong to Christ, that brother is your business. It’s easy to talk about community, but it’s harder to live it when confrontation is required. Yet the call of Jesus is clear: leave the ninety-nine and go after the one. That’s the heart of God.

Restoring a brother may not always be well-received. It might cost you time, comfort, or reputation. But obedience is worth it. You don’t have to be a pastor or counselor. All God is asking you to do is care enough to act. Send the text. Make the call. Knock on the door. Sit across the table and speak truth seasoned with grace.

Brother, the same grace that pulled you out of wandering is the grace God wants to extend through you. Every time a man turns back to God, heaven rejoices. So don’t stand by and watch your brother drift. Go get him. And remember, you’re living proof that grace still brings men home.

Application Questions

1. Is there someone in your life right now who’s drifting from God’s truth?
2. What holds you back from stepping in to help restore a wandering brother?
3. How has God used others to bring you back when you were off course?
4. What does loving correction look like in your relationships?

A Prayer for Your Day

Lord, give me courage to pursue the men who are drifting from You. Help me love enough to tell the truth and to fight for their restoration. Remind me of the grace You’ve shown me, and let that same grace flow through my words and actions. Use me to bring a brother home. Amen.

ABOUT THE AUTHOR

RICK BURGESS is the host of the nationally syndicated radio show, *The Rick Burgess Show*. (He previously co-hosted *The Rick and Bubba Show* for thirty-one years). He has authored *Men Don't Run In the Rain: A Son's Reflections on Life, Faith, and an Iconic Father*, *Sin Always Matters: The Cost of Sin and the Power of Grace* and *Transformed: Embracing the Death of Self and the Power of God*, as well as co-authoring multiple New York Times bestselling books and the *How to Be a Man* series of devotionals. As a commentator and guest, Rick has appeared on various radio and television shows, including *Fox and Friends* and *The Sean Hannity Show*. Rick is a frequent speaker at church services and marriage conferences, but his true passion is men's ministry. As founder of *The Man Church* (themanchurch.com), Rick calls on the modern church to put into practice what they say every Father's Day, that a man's family will follow him if he leads them.

Rick and his wife Sherri were married in 1996, have five children, and reside in Birmingham, Alabama. Rick's Spirit-filled message at their youngest son's memorial service was the most-watched video on YouTube in the world the week it was posted. Find out more about their ministry by going to burgessministries.com.